Feel the Beat

Seasonal Movement and Activity Songs for Grades K-3

By John Jacobson
and Roger Emerson

T0085211

TABLE OF CONTENTS

Teaching objectives linked to the National Standards are provided for each song in this collection. The complete National Arts Standards and additional materials relating to the Standards are available from MENC at **www.menc.org.**

7777 W. Bluemound Rd. P.O. Box 13819 Milwaukee, WI 53213

Visit Hal Leonard Online at
www.halleonard.com

Feel the Beat

Teaching Objectives and National Standards for "Feel the Beat"

- Sing in tune and maintain a steady beat, responding to conductor cues
- Identify repeated melodic/rhythmic patterns
- Identify verse and refrain
- Demonstrate steady beat through body percussion
- Demonstrate phrase structure by clapping at the end of a phrase

This lesson addresses the National Standards for Music ***K–4*** *Education: 1b, 1e, 5c, 6a, 6b, 6c, 6e, 9a.*

Get Ready...

There are so many possibilities to celebrate and learn using the song "Feel the Beat." It's a great song to start a new school year since "beat" is a pretty good place to start the musical year. Once you feel and understand the beat, the other elements of music often start to make sense and become internalized.

Get Set...

Whack Attacks: This is simply a term I use to describe almost any body percussion routine you want to incorporate. Here's a very simple example:

Beat	Action
1	Clap
2	Snap fingers of R hand
3	Snap fingers of L hand
4	Clap again

Repeat over and over. Notice that when you do so, there will be two claps together (4 and 1). So as you teach it, you might speak, "Clap, snap, snap, clap. Clap, snap, snap, clap. Clap..."

Another simple version would be:

Beat	Action
1	Clap
2	Pat R leg
3	Pat L leg
4	Clap again

A more advanced Whack Attack might combine the two:

Beat	Action
1	Clap
2	Pat R leg
3	Pat L leg
4	Clap again
5	Snap fingers of R hand
6	Snap fingers of L hand
7	Clap again
8	Clap again*

*Notice on this version there are three claps in the middle as you repeat it.

Now if you want to get even more advanced, try this:

Beat	Action
1	Clap
2	Pat R leg
3	Pat L leg
4	Clap again
5	Hit L foot with R hand behind your back
6	Pat L leg with L hand
7	Pat R leg with R hand
8	Clap
9	Hit R foot with L hand behind your back
10	Pat R leg with R hand
11	Pat L leg with L hand
12	Clap
13	Snap fingers of R hand
14	Snap fingers of L hand
15	Clap
16	Clap

Go...

Now divide the class into three or four groups and do all of these Whack Attacks simultaneously during the refrain of "Feel the Beat." You could also make up your own Whack Attacks. Combine them with singers who simply clap on or off the beats and so on. You might even add classroom percussion instruments and tap dancers to the cacophony for a real showstopper!

Feel the Beat

Words and Music by
John Jacobson and Roger Emerson

VERSE 1
If you find you're feelin' low,
And you don't know where to go,
Get up off your seat and feel the beat.
When you want to run and hide,
Listen to the rhythm down deep inside.
Got to move your feet and feel the beat.

REFRAIN
Feel the beat from your head down to
your feet.
Feel the beat.
Everybody clap your hands!
Feel the beat.
Every beat can be so sweet.
Feel the beat.
Everybody clap your hands!

VERSE 2
When the music overflows,
From your hair down to your toes,
Let 'er rip, let's skip and feel the beat.
When you don't know where to start,
Feel the rhythm movin' down in your
heart.
Take a chance,
Come dance and feel the beat.

REFRAIN
Feel the beat from your head down to
your feet.
Feel the beat.
Everybody clap your hands!
Feel the beat.
Every beat can be so sweet.
Feel the beat.
Everybody clap your hands!
Everybody clap your hands!
Everybody clap your hands!
Everybody clap your hands!

(Dance Break)

Feel the beat from your head down to
your feet.
Feel the beat.
Everybody clap your hands!
Everybody clap your hands!
Everybody clap your hands!
Everybody clap your hands!
(spoken) I'm beat!

Feel the Beat

Words and Music by JOHN JACOBSON
and ROGER EMERSON

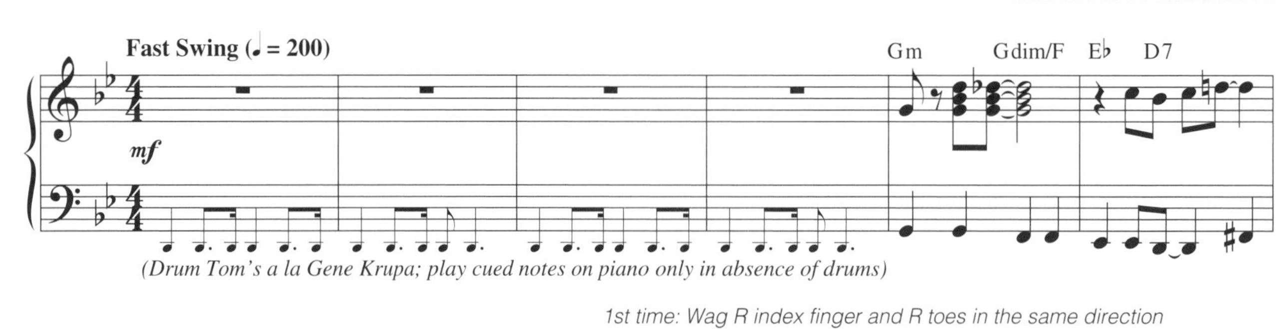

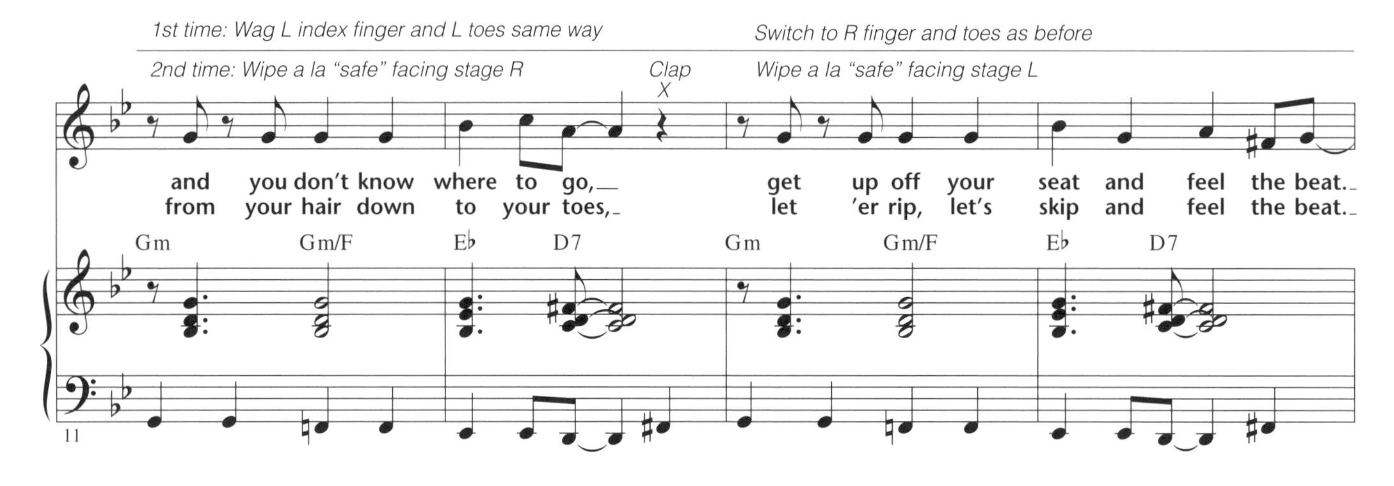

* 8 count Whack Attack: 1. Clap, 2. Pat R leg, 3. Pat L leg, 4. Clap, 5. Snap R, 6. Snap L, 7-8: Clap twice

* Try creating your own variations of Whack Attacks so there are several different patterns being performed simultaneously.

Repeat 5 times
D.S. al Coda
Repeat 5 times
CODA
Wipe
mp
cresc.
clap
Wipe
mf
Ev - 'ry-bod - y clap your hands!
Ev - 'ry-bod - y clap your hands!
D7(♭9)
Wipe
f
Wipe a la "safe"
Wipe off brow like "Whew!"
One final clap on the stinger note
Ev - 'ry-bod - y clap your hands! I'm beat!
Gm

The Boogie Ooogie Woogie!

Teaching Objectives and National Standards for "The Boogie Ooogie Woogie!"

- Sing in tune and maintain a steady beat
- Identify repeated melodic patterns
- Identify verse and refrain
- Clap on off beats
- Discuss characteristics of Jazz and Boogie Woogie style music

*This lesson addresses the National Standards for Music **K–4** Education: 1b, 1c, 1e, 5c, 6a, 6b, 6c, 7b, 9a.*

Get Ready...

Here's a song that will get your heart going. Well, at least it got mine going! So, to get ready, clear the decks and warn the neighbors, especially if you live on an upper floor. (You'll know what I mean when you get to the stomping part.)

There aren't any complicated dance moves, but one you might not know is the Sugar Foot. For a proper Sugar Foot, all you have to do is stand on the balls of your feet and twist your heels back and forth, both in the same direction. If you want, you can even walk in place or move around simply by stepping with each twist of the heels. That's a little more challenging. Don't think about it too much, and the sheer energy of the move could make it happen. Also, when you do the Sugar Foot, you can shimmy your Jazz Hands at about head level, or wiggle your index fingers if that's more your style.

Get Set...

As you can see, the moves suggested for the refrain are as repetitive as the refrain itself. In the choreography notes, I suggest that you make the claps and the snaps on the off beats . . . in other words, after you sing the word. But if you find it easier to do the moves at the same time as you sing the corresponding word, that's okay too. Indeed, the stomps should land right on the word "stomp" and can be with one or both feet.

Another way to spice it up a bit is to do each repetition of the words "Clap, snap and stomp" facing a different wall.

Still another option, which is a lot of fun, is to partner up. Then when you get to the refrain, you do the first "Clap, snap, stomp, boogie woogie" facing downstage, the second set facing your partner, the third set facing upstage, and the fourth set facing back to back with your partner.

For your more advanced performers, you might even add some simple Jitterbug or Swing style dance moves during one of the refrains.

At the bridge section, you might try having a third of the group clapping, a third of the group snapping, and a third of the group stomping throughout.

Go...

Have a lot of fun. There are no mistakes or wrong moves in "The Boogie Ooogie Woogie," which we, of course, all know translates to "Music Is My Life!"

The Boogie Ooogie Woogie!

Words and Music by
John Jacobson and Roger Emerson

VERSE 1

When you get in trouble and don't know what to do,
Feelin' kind of mellow and feelin' kind of blue,
Don't give up! Get on down!
Do this dance all over town.
Boogie Ooogie Woogie and bring a friend or two.

REFRAIN

All you do is:
Clap! Snap! Stomp! Boogie Woogie!
Clap! Snap! Stomp! Ooogie Boogie!
Clap! Snap! Stomp! Woogie Boogie!
Clap! Snap! Stomp! Ooogie Woogie!
Boogie Ooogie Woogie and dance 'til dawn with me!
(shout) Come on now!
Clap! Snap! Stomp! Boogie Woogie!
Clap! Snap! Stomp! Ooogie Boogie!
Clap! Snap! Stomp! Woogie Boogie!
Clap! Snap! Stomp! Ooogie Woogie!
Boogie Ooogie Woogie and dance 'til dawn with me!

VERSE 2

Everybody's doing it,
'Cause there is nothin' to it, you see.
Easy as the alphabet; easy as one, two, three.
A B C! One, two, three! I got you and you got me.
Boogie Ooogie Woogie, now don't forget Do Re Mi.

REPEAT REFRAIN

Body Percussion Break

REPEAT REFRAIN

With me!

The Boogie Ooogie Woogie!

Words and Music by JOHN JACOBSON
and ROGER EMERSON

1st time: Twist L foot back and forth with heel up
2nd time: Thumbs to self then point out, then return thumbs to self
Do the Twist
Do this dance all o - ver town.
I got you and you got me.
Boo - gie Ooo - gie Woo - gie and
Boo - gie Ooo - gie Woo - gie now
F7
E♭7
B♭7
15
2 step claps
Stop
bring a friend or two.
don't for - get Do Re Mi.
All you do is:
All you do is:
F7
18
These two measures can be done facing a different wall each time
Clap X
Snap X
Hop on both feet
Sugarfoot
Repeat mm. 21-22
Clap! Snap! Stomp! Boo - gie Woo - gie! Clap! Snap!
B♭9
21
Repeat mm. 21-22
Stomp! Ooo - gie Boo - gie! Clap! Snap! Stomp! Woo - gie Boo - gie!
E♭13
24

Repeat mm. 21-22
Continue Sugarfoot
Clap! Snap! Stomp! Ooo-gie Woo-gie! Boo-gie Ooo-gie Woo-gie and
B♭9
F7
27
Step clap 2 times
Stop
Shouted: "Come on now!"
dance 'til dawn with me!
E♭13
B♭9
(F7 implied)
30
Repeat mm. 21-22
Repeat mm. 21-22
Clap! Snap! Stomp! Boo-gie Woo-gie! Clap! Snap! Stomp! Ooo-gie Boo-gie!
B♭9
33
Repeat mm. 21-22
Repeat mm. 21-22
Clap! Snap! Stomp! Woo-gie Boo-gie! Clap! Snap! Stomp! Ooo-gie Woo-gie!
E♭13
B♭9
37

Continue Sugarfoot
(3rd time) To Coda
Step clap twice
Stop
Boo-gie Ooo-gie Woo-gie and dance 'til dawn with me!
F7
E♭13
B♭9
(F7 implied)
Claps
Snaps
N.C.
mf
cresc. poco a poco
Clap
Snap
Stomp
Shouted: Clap, snap, stomp, let's go!
Stomps
D.S. al Coda
CODA
Step clap 4 times
Wipe brow with R hand like "whew!"
Thumbs to self
With me!
B♭9
A7(♯5)
A♭13
G7
G♭maj7
N.C.

Scarecrow Scat

Teaching Objectives and National Standards for "Scarecrow Scat"

- Sing in tune, maintaining a steady beat and responding to conductor cues
- Identify verse and refrain
- Identify Call and Response
- Read and perform dynamics (mf, f, cresc)
- Explore scat singing and question/answer improvisation on unpitched instruments

This lesson addresses the National Standards for Music ***K–4*** *Education: 1a, 1b, 1c, 1e, 3a, 5c, 6a, 6b, 6c, 7b, 9a.*

Get Ready...

This is not your grandmother's scarecrow. This is the coolest scarecrow in the garden! It will be lots of fun to pretend to be this scarecrow or to just dance along with him or her. Of course, if you want to perform the song in a concert, you could add the obvious costuming ideas: bib overalls full of patches, a straw hat, a bandana, a plaid shirt with pieces of straw sticking out from various places and so on. Or, you could have one person play the scarecrow and the rest of the class dress up like crows. This would be a fun addition to a fall program either by itself or combined with songs of the harvest, Thanksgiving, pumpkins, autumn, a hoedown and so on.

Get Set...

The scarecrows starts with his/her arms stretched out to the sides as if hanging on a garden fence post. Another option is to run a stick through the jacket of the scarecrow so that it looks like their arms are stuck straight out to the side. They are actually inside your costume.

The dance moves are fairly simple and can be performed in quite a small space. Sway snaps and flopping hands make up the bulk of the refrain. If you have some cast members playing crows, they can add a lot of flapping of wings to get their blood moving.

During the dance break, the scarecrow could pretend to play a saxophone and/or chase the crows around the stage, always in the feel of the music.

Once you have learned the song, you might encourage the scarecrow to vary the scat riffs that he sings and make it true improvisation. The chorus would try to match what the scarecrow sang. You could even replace the scatting with body percussion or dance moves to be mimicked by the rest of the cast. For instance, on one lick, the scarecrow could spin around, then the cast spins. The scarecrow could hop on one foot, and then the cast does the same. Skipping, jumping, sliding, twisting and any other moves that reflect the music would be good for the scarecrow to challenge the others to do.

Go...

Try adding classroom instruments to the scatting part of the song. The scarecrow (leader) could play a lick or a note on a musical instrument and the rest of the cast could try to imitate it. For instance, he might play the "ba doo ba doo ba doo wah" rhythm on a drum or box, and then the cast would echo it. He could play a pattern on sticks or a triangle and the others could try to imitate it and so on.

Have fun. There are no limits to what you can imagine with the brain of a scarecrow!

Scarecrow Scat

Words and Music by
John Jacobson and Roger Emerson

VERSE 1
Hangin' around the picket fence,
The garden's number one defense.
Let me sing a thing or two.
I've got a single job to do.

VERSE 2
Standing in the summer sun,
I'm not allowed to have much fun.
A scarecrow never says a word,
But I'll sing some scat to scare that bird!

REFRAIN (Leader/Echo)
Ba doo ba doo bah doo wee! (echo)
Ba doo ba doo bah doo wah! (echo)
Ba doo ba doo bah doo wee! (echo)
Ba doo ba doo bah doo wah! (echo)
Ba doo ba doo bah doo whoa! (echo)
I'm gonna scare that crow! (echo)
Ba doo ba doo bah doo whoa! (echo)
I'm gonna scare that crow! (echo)

VERSE 3
Man, there ought to be a law.
I've got a head made out of straw.
So I'm hanging on a stick,
Singing out my favorite lick!

REPEAT REFRAIN

Dance Break

REPEAT REFRAIN

Scarecrow Scat

Words and Music by JOHN JACOBSON
and ROGER EMERSON

Hold arms straight out to the sides like a scarecrow hanging on a stick.

Em7 F♯m7 Em7 F♯m7

13

1st & 2nd times: Resume tilting with arms extended.
cresc.
scare - crow nev - er says a word_ but I'll sing some scat to scare_ that bird!_
So I'm hang - ing on a stick,_ sing - ing out my fav - o - rite lick!_
Em7
F♯m7
Em7
cresc.
17
Kids
Sing all 3 times
Tilt and snap
f
Ba doo ba doo bah doo wee!_
Leader
Tilt and snap
f
Ba doo ba doo bah doo wee!_
B7(♯9)
Em11
f
21
Tilt and snap then add Jazz hands on "wah"
Ba doo ba doo bah doo wah!_
Tilt and snap then add Jazz hands on "wah"
Ba doo ba doo bah doo wah!_
Swivel knees both in the same direction
Ba doo ba doo bah doo wee!_
24

Swivel knees both in the same direction
Jazz hands
Ba doo ba doo bah doo wee!
Ba doo ba doo bah doo wah!
Jazz hands
Ba doo ba doo bah doo wah!
Am11
Em11
27
Push hands from facing self to out as if trying to keep balance.
Ba doo ba doo ba doo whoa!
Push hands from facing self to out as if trying to keep balance.
Thumbs to self
Ba doo ba doo ba doo whoa!
I'm gon - na scare that crow!
Bm11
30
Thumbs to self
Claw hands
Repeat mm. 31-34
I'm gon - na scare that crow!
Ba doo ba doo bah doo whoa!
Claw hands
Repeat mm. 30-33
Ba doo ba doo bah doo whoa!
Em11
Bm11
33

1, 2
I'm gon - na scare that crow!
I'm gon - na scare that crow!
Em7
F♯m7
36
Em7
F♯m7
39
3
Thumbs to self
I'm gon - na scare that crow!
I'm gon - na scare that crow!
Claw hands
Jazz hands out to sides
Claw hands
rit.
rit.
BOO!
BOO!
B7(♭5♭9)
rit.
42

Tumblin' Down

Teaching Objectives and National Standards for "Tumblin' Down"

- Sing in tune, maintaining a steady beat and responding to conductor cues
- Respond through movement to melodic direction
- Identify verse and refrain
- Sing dynamics (mf, f)
- Compare and contrast repeated melodic/rhythmic lines

*This lesson addresses the National Standards for Music **K–4** Education: 1b, 1e, 5c, 6a, 6b, 6c, 6e.*

Get Ready...

To begin this fun classroom game, have all of the students divide up into three equal groups: 1. The Leaves, 2. The Nuts (or acorns if you're cautious about calling a kid a nut), and 3. The Snow (or the "flakes" if you aren't cautious at all.) Here is an easy way to divide up: Put an equal amount of each group name on pieces of paper and have each student draw one out of a hat. Once they have their assigned group, they can join that group in one area of the room like a three-ringed circus.

Get Set...

The three groups each form a circle and sit down. During the verse, the group in focus (leaves, then nuts, then snow) stands up and walks in a circle to the beat of the music. If they want to act out their part, they should *ad lib* as desired. When you get to the part "all the ______ come tumblin' down" whichever verse it is, those circlers slowly tumble to the ground. Instruct the students to fall gently like falling leaves, snow or nuts that land on soft leaves. They scramble to their feet and do it again for the repeat of the verse. Another option is have the entire group participate in the second time through each verse. In this case there would be more activity for each group throughout without so much "down" time."

During the second half of the last verse, everyone would be moving in a circle and then would fall down at the appropriate time for the last few lines. In other words, first the leaves fall, then the nuts, then the snow.

During the refrain, the entire class can slowly tumble to the ground, or the teacher can randomly point to a circle. When they do so, that circle tumbles to the ground.

Here is another option: Have the circles one inside the other as opposed to scattered around the room. This will make it possible to play the song/game in a more confined place.

Go...

If you choose to perform the song for an audience, you could line up the three groups, keeping them with their fellow leaves, nuts or flakes. They could all simply sway during the verse part and then the appropriate group can tumble down at the end of the verse. During the refrain, simply use your L "rain" hand to move from high to low, then your R "rain" hand, then both.

Tumblin' Down

Words and Music by
John Jacobson and Roger Emerson

VERSE 1

I am a leaf. When the cold wind blows,
I hang on tight, but must let go;
And all the leaves come tumblin' down.

I am a leaf. When the cold wind blows,
I hang on tight, but must let go;
And all the leaves come tumblin' down.

Tumblin', tumblin', tumblin', tumblin',
All the leaves come tumblin' down.

VERSE 2

I'm just a nut. I hang on but,
When autumn calls, I have to fall;
And all the nuts come tumblin' down.

I'm just a nut. I hang on but,
When autumn calls, I have to fall;
And all the nuts come tumblin' down.

Tumblin', tumblin', tumblin', tumblin',
All the nuts come tumblin' down.

VERSE 3

Oh, you should know I am the snow.
I get so bold when it gets cold;
And all the snow comes tumblin' down.

Oh, you should know I am the snow.
I get so bold when it gets cold;
And all the snow comes tumblin' down.

Tumblin', tumblin', tumblin', tumblin',
All the leaves come tumblin',
All the nuts come tumblin',
All the snow comes tumblin' down.

4 / 16

Tumblin' Down

Words and Music by JOHN JACOBSON
and ROGER EMERSON

hang on tight but must let go; and all the leaves come tum - blin'
au - tumn calls I have to fall; and all the nuts come tum - blin'
F/B♭ C Gm7 B♭ F/C C
17
Circle 2 gently tumbles to the ground
Both circles walk in a circle
down.
down.
Tum - blin',
Tum - blin',
F B♭2/F F B♭2/F F B♭2/F F F/A B♭ F
21
tum - blin', tum - blin', tum - blin', all the leaves come tum - blin'
tum - blin', tum - blin', tum - blin', all the nuts come tum - blin'
C F B♭ F C Dm Gm7 F/B Csus C
26
Both circles gently tumble to the ground
down.
down.
2. I'm
3. Oh,
F B♭2/F F B♭2/F F B♭2/F F F
31

Circle 1 stands and does motions while Circle 2 watches
Point at audience
Thumbs to self
Show muscles
Hug self and shiver
you should know I am the snow; I get so bold when it gets cold; and
G2
C/E
G/C
D
f
36
Snow hands
Circle 1 melts to the ground while Circle 2 stands
all the snow comes tum - blin' down.
Am7
C
G/D
D
G
C2/G
G
C2/G
40
Circle 2 does motions; Circle 1 watches
Point to audience
Thumbs to self
Oh, you should know I am the snow; I
G
C2/G
G
G2
C/E
44
Show muscles
Hug self and shiver
get so bold when it gets cold; and all the snow comes tum - blin'
G/C
D
Am7
C
G/D
D
48

Circle 2 snow hands and melt to the ground
All stand and walk in circles
down.
Tum - blin',
G C2/G G C2/G G C2/G G G/B C G
52
Circle 1 tumbles down
tum - blin', tum - blin', tum - blin', all the leaves come tum - blin',
D G C G D Em Am7 G/C Dsus D
57
Circle 2 tumbles down
all the nuts come tum - blin', all the snow comes tum –
Am7 G/C Dsus D Am7 G/C Dsus
62
All do snow hands
rit.
All remain on the ground (option: make snow angels)
blin' down.
D G C2/G G C2/G G C2/G G
rit.
66

Papa's on the Housetop

Teaching Objectives and National Standards for "Papa's on the Housetop"

- Sing in tune, maintaining a steady beat and responding to conductor
- Identify repeated sections
- Sing dynamics (mf, f)
- Identify syncopation

*This lesson addresses the National Standards for Music **K–4** Education: 1b, 1c, 1e, 5a, 5c, 6, 9a.*

Get Ready...

Bless their hearts! Many dads really try their best to make our rooftops fantastic with holiday lights. But what makes them think that all of a sudden, once a year, they are going to have an artistic flare, where your home and front yard are going to miraculously be the envy of the neighborhood full of twinkling lights and audio-animatronics? Oh well, you ought to give them an "A" for effort and at least encourage them to be safe as they make their annual trip to the chimney tops to spread their holiday cheer.

To honor them, (or poke loving fun) we wrote this parody called "Papa's on the Housetop" to make children giggle and dads chuckle at themselves. If you decide to perform this selection in a program, you might actually sing a verse and refrain of the traditional carol as a set-up to this new version. You could also dress up the cast as children playing outside on a cold winter day, while Dad does his best to trim the house with lights. You might include a nurse or paramedic in the cast as well, just in case.

Get Set...

You should be able to figure out the choreography suggestions without much trouble. Check out my rendition above the piano accompaniment on pp. 28-32. Here are some moves you may not recognize.

"Home Alone" hands come from the holiday movie of the same name. Just hold your face in both hands and look worried.

The slow slides in measures 22 and 23 are supposed to look as though you are sliding around on a slippery slope.

Ham it up on the introduction and interlude sections, talking to one another and pointing to the rooftop as though watching Papa nervously and telling each other how afraid you are that he is going to hurt himself.

In a production, you might end with a comic bit of one cast member shouting something like, "Okay Dad! Looks great! Plug it in!" At which point, the stage lights could flicker and go out with a sizzling sound.

Go...

If "Papa" doesn't work for you, feel free to change the lyric to Daddy, Da-ad, or completely go with a different character like "Granny" or "Mama."

Most importantly, have a good time and don't forget to thank your papa for all of his effort!

Papa's on the Housetop

Based on the tune "Up on the Housetop"
Arranged with New Words and Music by
John Jacobson and Roger Emerson

VERSE 1

Papa's on the housetop stringin' up lights,
Try'n to get ready for one big night.
The roof is covered with ice and snow.
Papa's up, look out below!

REFRAIN

Papa, no! Please don't go!
Papa, no! Please don't go
Up on the housetop like Saint Nick!
That icy roof is, oh, so slick!

VERSE 2

Each and every year he does his best,
Santa's sleigh and all the rest.
Blow up snowmen ten feet tall,
Maybe they will break his fall!

REPEAT REFRAIN

VERSE 3

Papa's tangled up in an awful mess.
Better send an S.O.S.
He's getting near the satellite dish,
"Get down safely," is my wish!

repeat Verse 1

REPEAT REFRAIN

Dad, I love that neon star.
Papa, you're the best by far!

Papa's on the Housetop

Based on the tune: "Up on the Housetop"
Arranged with New Words and Music by
JOHN JACOBSON and ROGER EMERSON

Home Alone
Begging hands
Home Alone
Begging hands
Pa - pa, no! Please_ don't go! Pa - pa, no! Please_ don't go___
F Gm7 F/A C G/B Am7 G Am7 G/B C G/B C/E
15
Point up
Hold stomach as though chubby
Slow slide to the L
up on the house-top like Saint Nick! That i - cy roof is oh,
C C/B♭ F/A C/G F C/E Am7 Dm7
19
Slide to the R
1 Pretend to slip
Resume pointing up and looking afraid for Papa
so slick!
G7sus C5
23
2 Pretend to slip
slick!
G7sus Cm
27

Wrap arms around self as though in a straight jacket
3. Pa - pa's tan-gled up in an aw - ful mess._ Bet - ter send an
Cm Cm/B♭ A♭maj7 Cm/G Fm Fm/E♭
"S. O. S."__ He's get-ting near the sat - el - lite dish._
Home Alone
Dm7(♭5) G7 Cm Cm/B♭ A♭maj7 Cm/G
Cup hands around mouth as though calling
Prayer hands
"Get down safe - ly," is my wish!
Fm Fm/E♭ Dm7(♭5) G7 Cm A7
Same as first verse Hand Jive
Travel hands and present high
Hand Jive
1. Pa - pa's on the house - top string-in' up lights,_ try - in' to get read - y for
D D/C♯ Bm7 D/A G Em7

Point R index finger
Home Alone
one big night._ The roof is cov-ered with ice and snow._
G/A D D/C♯ Bm7 D/A
43
Point up
Calling hands
Pa - pa's up, look out be - low!
G Em7 G2/A D A/D G/D D/F♯
46
Home Alone
Beg
Home Alone
Pa - pa, no! Please_ don't go! Pa - pa, no! Please_
G Am7 G/B D A/C♯ Bm7 A7 G/B A7/C♯ D
50
Beg
Point up
Hold stomach
_ don't go_ up on the house - top like Saint Nick!
A/E D/F♯ D D/C G/B D/A G
53

Slide L
Slide R
That i - cy roof is oh, so slick! Dad, I love that
D/F♯ Bm7 Em7 G/A D D D/C
56
Roll your eyes
Start Hand Jive
Scoop L hand
ne - on star. Pa - pa, you're the best
G/B D/A G D/F♯ Bm7 Em7
59
Scoop R hand
Applaud from high to low
Thumbs up
and look up
by far!
G/A D
62

Jammin' in our Jammies

Teaching Objectives and National Standards for "Jammin' in our Jammies"

- Sing in tune, maintaining a steady beat and responding to conductor
- Sing and read mi so la
- Analyze familiar melodies
- Sing dynamics (mp, mf, f)
- Demonstrate steady beat through body percussion

*This lesson addresses the National Standards for Music **K–4** Education: 1b, 1c, 1e, 5b, 5c, 6e, 9a.*

Get Ready...

Here's a high-energy dance that ought to get your day started or keep you awake at night. Ideally, the kids would be dressed in some form of pajamas if you were going to perform it for a holiday concert. This could include bathrobes, funny slippers or traditional pajamas. They could be worn right over their other clothes. You could even opt to simply have pajama tops be the costume or even just imagine the whole thing. Another option would be to don nightcaps or any combination of all the above. Most kids probably have decent pajamas they could wear, but you would want to be discreet in finding out if some need to be provided. You can always just wear shorts and T-shirts. Indeed, you might absolutely want to wear shorts and T-shirts underneath the P.J.s for obvious reasons. In the end, don't worry too much about costumes. It's just a "for fun " song.

Get Set...

There are some dance steps suggested in the choreography notes above the piano accompaniment on p. 37 that you may not know. Why would you? I just made them up! You might come up with your own version of them, but here are my suggestions.

The Candy Cane: Reach one arm over head with a bent elbow and wrist. With feet together, nod your head twice L, twice R, twice L, twice R.

The Jingle Bell Twist: The same as the Twist but you might have some bells to jingle in your hands.

The Christmas Tree: Hold your fingers together overhead like the point of tree and sway your hips LRL, RLR.

The Mistletoe: Hug yourself and twist from the waist while looking up with your backs to the audience, like you are being hugged, then wipe your hands down your sides as you say "eew!"

Go...

Perform this song with a lot of energy. If there are students who want a different role, put together a pajama air band and let them pretend to "jam" as they play air guitars, drums and bass. It's a jam fest! Have fun!

Jammin' in our Jammies

Words and Music by
John Jacobson and Roger Emerson

INTRODUCTION
One fine winter morning,
When I opened up my eyes,
Gathered in my living room
Was a big surprise.
All my friends were gathered there
At the crack of dawn.
So we had a party with our pajamas on!

VERSE 1
Jammin' in our jammies,
Having us a holiday!
Jammin' in our jammies,
Everybody shout hooray! *(Hooray!)*
Mama in her nightgown,
Daddy in his flannel pants.
Santa is the D.J., spinnin' in his P.J.s now!
Let's dance!
Let's dance!
Let's dance!
Let's dance!

VERSE 2
Jammin' in our jammies
Makes a holiday complete.
Jammin' in our jammies,
Fuzzy wuzzies on our feet! *(Sweet!)*
Mama in her nightgown,
Daddy in his flannel pants.
Santa is the D.J., spinnin' in his P.J.s now!
Let's dance!
Let's dance!
Let's dance!
Let's dance!

DANCE BREAK
(spoken) Do the Candy Cane!
(spoken) Do the Jingle Bell Twist!
(spoken) Do the Christmas Tree!
(spoken) Do the Mistletoe (eew!)

Santa is the D.J., spinnin' in his P.J.s now!
Let's dance!
Let's dance!
Let's dance!
Let's dance!

Jammin' in our Jammies

Words and Music by JOHN JACOBSON
and ROGER EMERSON

1st time: Do the Twist
2nd time: Air guitar
Both times Mashed Potato
2 R
2 L
mf
1. Jam-min' in our jam-mies, hav-ing us a hol - i - day!
2. Jam-min' in our jam-mies makes a hol - i - day com-plete.
D G/D D G/D D A D/A A D/A A
14
1st time: Do the Twist
2nd time: Air guitar
Both times:
Step slap
L X R X
1st: Clap, then present high
2nd: Clap, then wipe "safe"
Jam-min' in our jam-mies, ev-'ry-bod - y shout hoo-ray!
Jam-min' in our jam-mies; fuz-zie wuz-zies on our feet!
1st time shout: Hooray!
2nd time shout: Sweet!
D G/D D G/D D A G/A A G/A A
18
Peppermint Twist
Rubber legs and swing lower arms in circles,
elbows fastened to hips 4 times
Ma-ma in her night gown; dad-dy in his flan - nel pants.
D G/D D G/D D A D/A A D/A A
22
Hand Jive
Traveling hands
from low to high
Present high
f
San-ta is the D. J., spin-nin' in his P. J.s now!
Let's dance!
G D/F♯ Em7 G/D A/C♯ Bm7 A
26

Sugarfoot
Twist while squatting
Let's dance!
Let's dance!
D Em7 D/F♯ G A7 G/B D Em7 D/F♯ G A7 G/B D
Butterfly
(3rd time)
To Coda
Swing both hands overhead like they are both swinging a lasso
Let's dance!
Em7 D/F♯ G A7 G/B Asus A
See teacher note p. 33 for description of these dances.
(2nd time) D.S. al Coda
Spoken: Do the Candy Cane!
Spoken: Do the Christmas Tree!
Spoken: Do the Jingle Bell Twist
Spoken: Do the Mistletoe (eew!)
CODA
Clap X
Present high
Let's dance!
A7 G/B A/C♯ D

Slippery!

Teaching Objectives and National Standards for "Slippery"

- Sing in tune, maintaining a steady beat and responding to conductor
- Maintain a steady beat on a percussion instrument
- Identify verse and refrain
- Demonstrate the flow of 6/8 meter through movement

This lesson addresses the National Standards for Music ***K–4*** *Education: 1b, 1e, 2a, 2e, 6a, 6c, 6e.*

Get Ready...

This song should be great fun as long as nobody gets too wild! It's fun to pretend to be on a slippery sidewalk and see if you can really make it look like you are barely able to stand up. I would suggest that you set a few ground rules before you do the actions that are recommended in the piano accompaniment or try out your own.

Rule #1: Nobody can touch anybody or anything when you start slipping around the room.

Rule #2: Everybody should stop moving when you get to the end of the refrain and recover for the next section.

Now rules are not always a lot of fun. So I suggest you make them more so by creating a pledge that everybody has to repeat before you do the song. For instance, you might say,

Repeat after me:

I promise that during the "Slippery" song
I will not touch anybody or anything, except the floor.
When the teacher says stop, we'll all stop.
When the song is over, we'll forget all about slipping.
But for now, let's have some fun!

Get Set...

Slide whistles would be a good addition to this song. If you could get a hold of at least three of them (or any combination of threes), you could have the slide whistle play on the "Whoop! Whoop! Whoops!" Let the players be creative with the sounds that the slide whistles can make. Each group of slide whistlers would play on one whoop, or all of the slide whistlers could try to play three whoops in a row by moving their slider in a bit on each one.

The spoken "whoops" should be as if you are about to fall on the ice. As you do the accompanying move of standing on one foot, you should pretend to be very wobbly but not fall down completely.

If you wanted, you could fall down at the end of each refrain, then quickly stand up to start all over again.

You might also add some wood blocks or another percussion instrument to accompany the verse sections with a simple walking pattern.

Go...

If the song is not performed for an audience, but only in the classroom or gymnasium, the singers would not all have to be facing the front. You could move in a circle around the room like skaters on an ice rink.

Warning! Once you introduce this song to your students, they may want to do it all the time. It's a "Slippery" slope!

Slippery!

Words and Music by
John Jacobson and Roger Emerson

VERSE 1

One day not long ago, I was walking through the snow,
Feeling mighty fine and rather "chippery"!   *(spoken) "Chippery?"*
Oh, but things were not so nice when I hit a patch of ice,
And every step I took was very slippery!

REFRAIN

Slippery!   *(spoken) Whoop! Whoop! Whoop!*
Slippery!   *(spoken) Whoop! Whoop! Whoop!*
The whole wide world got slippery!
Slippery!   *(spoken) Whoop! Whoop! Whoop!*
Slippery!   *(spoken) Whoop! Whoop! Whoop!*
The whole wide world got slippery!

VERSE 2

Oh, it's very plain to see, on a winter walk with me,
We can step in style in our "frippery"!   *(spoken) "Frippery?"*
Let's put on our winter suits and don't forget your boots,
For winter walks are often very slippery!

REFRAIN

Slippery!   *(spoken) Whoop! Whoop! Whoop!*
Slippery!   *(spoken) Whoop! Whoop! Whoop!*
The whole wide world got slippery!
Slippery!   *(spoken) Whoop! Whoop! Whoop!*
Slippery!   *(spoken) Whoop! Whoop! Whoop!*
The whole wide world got slippery!

REPEAT REFRAIN

Slippery!

7 / 19

Words and Music by JOHN JACOBSON
and ROGER EMERSON

Both times: Wiggle knees
ev - 'ry step I took was ver - y slip - per - y!
win - ter walks are of - ten ver - y slip - per - y!
E♭
F7
B♭
B♭/D
17
Slide to the left and stand on L foot
Slide to the R and stand on R foot
(spoken) Whoop! Whoop! Whoop!
Whoop! Whoop! Whoop!
Slip - per - y!
Slip - per - y!
The
E♭
B♭/D
21
Pretend to walk on a slippery sidewalk
whole wide world got slip - per - y!
Cm7
F9
B♭
25
Repeat mm. 21-28
Whoop! Whoop! Whoop!
Whoop! Whoop! Whoop!
(3rd time) To Coda
Slip - per - y!
Slip - per - y!
The
E♭
B♭/D
29

whole wide world got slip - per - y!
Cm7
F9
B♭
Recover
2. Oh, it's slip-per - y!
Pretend to almost fall down
D.S. al Coda
CODA
Fall down
Whoop!

Walk the Valentine Line

Teaching Objectives and National Standards for "Walk the Valentine Line"

- Sing in tune, maintaining a steady beat and responding to conductor
- Sing in 2 parts, maintaining pitch and tempo
- Identify repeated melodic and rhythmic patterns
- Develop the ability to evaluate a rehearsal in musical terms

This lesson addresses the National Standards for Music ***K–4*** *Education: 1b, 1e, 5b, 6a, 6c, 7a.*

Get Ready...

Valentine's Day can be the most wonderful holiday or the loneliest, but it should never be the latter for a child in a music classroom. The most inclusive kind of dance I know of is the country line dance. Everyone can join in the fun and everybody comes away from it energized and feeling like a part of the club. I can still do the very first line dance I ever learned as a child standing next to my desk in music class. Whenever we had five minutes left of class, Mrs. Thomte would let us stand and dance the Alley Cat! We ALL loved it.

The best way to get ready for this line dance would be to clear away all the chairs and have the class line up in even rows like a parade formation. If you don't have a lot of room or time (like in Mrs. Thomte's class), simply stand up next to your desks or chairs, for this line dance does not take up a lot of room.

If you want to use the song in a program or even just reinforce the Valentine holiday theme, you could have each dancer hold a cutout of a heart in front of their chest as they dance. Then on the "Yeehaw," they could lift the heart over their heads in celebration.

Get Set...

Teach the dance slowly at the beginning of the class period. The steps are very simple and are written above the piano accompaniment on pages 45-48. You will quickly realize that any line dance you know will probably work with this song. For instance, The Electric Slide or Cotton Eye Joe work just as well.

After you have taught the steps, hand out red or white paper and have the students cut out a heart shape. You could then let them spend time decorating them using whatever materials you can gather. For the older students, you might have them draw a musical staff on the heart. Then, by using the note names of the lines and spaces, see who can come up with the most creative Valentine message on their staff by drawing in the notes and the corresponding letter names. This message could be one they want to say to a valentine or a reaction they might have if they receive a valentine. Allow them to use one, two or three letters that are not on the musical staff. For instance, they might notate B E A D E A and then add an R to spell out "Be A Dear!" or "Aa! Me!" or "Gee! Fun!" Another possibility would be to use the letters of the lines or spaces as the start of a phrase. Such as "Every Good Boy Does Fine." However, these messages should be "Valentine" in nature and the letters would not have to be in order. They might write "Do Be A Dear!" Or "Can any boy ever be good?"

A final choice would be for them to write a little melody and add a valentine phrase to it. Then, they could sing it, play on a keyboard and recite it, or pass it around the room. It could be as simple as two or three notes.

If all of this seems too complicated, or you want to perform the song for someone, you might have all of the students make a funny Valentine hat out of paper and other materials. Wear them as you do the dance.

Go...

Hold your hearts to your chest and finish the class off by "Walking the Valentine Line" again.

Walk the Valentine Line

Words and Music by
John Jacobson and Roger Emerson

VERSE 1

One fine day in February, something skips in my capillary.
Then I tell ya I just sorta get an ache in my aorta.
My heart goes boom; I clear the room.
I start to scoot in my dancin' boots.
Heel and toe, here we go; gotta take a chance.
Lined up now in a row; everybody dance!
Shake it left, shake it right; turn yourself about.
Dancing with my valentine makes me wanna shout!

REFRAIN

I'd walk the Valentine Line. (valentine line)
Walk the Valentine Line. (valentine line)
Won't you be mine (won't you be mine)
On the Valentine Line? (valentine line)
Won't you be mine (won't you be mine, be mine?)
On the Valentine Line?

VERSE 2

Once you find your valentine, step right up and get in line.
Join me now out on the floor.
You'll be mine and I'll be yours.
Our hearts go boom; we clear the room.
We start to scoot in our dancin' boots.
Heel and toe, here we go; gotta take a chance.
Lined up now in a row; everybody dance!
Shake it left, shake it right; turn yourself about.
Dancing with my valentine makes me wanna shout!

REPEAT REFRAIN

Won't you be mine?

Walk the Valentine Line

Words and Music by JOHN JACOBSON
and ROGER EMERSON

Step back with L foot, then R foot
Repeat m.13-14
Heels together toes apart and plié once
clear the room._ I start to scoot_ in my danc - in' boots.
clear the room._ We start to scoot_ in our danc - in' boots.
Em
F
D7/F♯
Gsus
G
14
L heel accent forward twice
Then L toes back twice
L heel forward once, back once
L heel forward again, then feet together
Heel and toe,_ here we go._ Got - ta take_ a chance._
F
C
G/B
Am7
C/G
18
Repeat mm.18-21 with R foot
Lined up now_ in a row,_ ev - 'ry-bod - y dance!_
F
D7
G
22
Stand on balls of feet and accent heels L, R, L
R, L, R
L, R, L
Spin R
Shake it left,_ shake it right,_ turn your-self_ a - bout._
F
C
G/B
Am7
C/G
26

Repeat mm. 26-28 with no spin
Danc - ing with my val - en - tine makes me wan - na shout!
F
D7
G
30
Leader
Walk forward 4 steps
L
R
L heel out front, then toes back, then heel out again, then pivot to face stage R.
I'd walk the Val-en-tine line. Walk the Val-en-tine line.
Kids (spoken)
(sing)
Yee haw! Val - en - tine line. Val - en - tine
C
D7
34
Back up moving toward stage L walking R, L, R, L
R heel out front, then toes back, then heel out again, then pivot to face front.)
Won't you be mine on the Val-en-tine line?
line. Won't you be mine? Val - en - tine
G7
C
38

Back up four steps
L, R, L, R
4-point Pivot
Won't you be mine on the Val-en-tine line?
line. Won't you be mine? Be mine?
G7
C
G/B
42
on the Val-en-tine
mine on the Val-en-tine
Am7
C/G
F
Gsus
G
C
46
Walk straight ahead 4 steps
rit.
Go to one knee and clasp
hands as though proposing.
line? Won't you be mine?
line? Won't you be mine?
F
C/E
Dm7
C
G/B
Am7
G
F
C
50

The Luck of the Irish

Teaching Objectives and National Standards for "The Luck of the Irish"

- Sing in tune and maintain a steady beat, responding to conductor cues
- Identify, read and sing melodic patterns with do re mi and so
- Recognize verses and refrain
- Sing dynamics (mf, f, cresc, ff)

*This lesson addresses the National Standards for Music **K–4** Education: 1b, 1c, 1e, 5b, 5c, 6a, 6b, 6c, 9a.*

Get Ready...

Here's a fun Irish song for those who want to wear green and sling the blarney around on Saint Patrick's Day or any time of the year.

The very first thing you need to try is whistle! Now, I know that a lot of younger children have a hard time whistling, in the same way they have a hard time snapping their fingers, but the effort can be a jovial event and need not be humiliating (especially if the teacher is willing to demonstrate their ineptness in front of the class.) I think it would be great to have an Irish whistling contest. The winner gets to whistle the solo in this song. Open the contest to the entire school. Your students could be the judges. I bet you'll be amazed at the turnout. I remember growing up and listening to the most wonderful whistling coming down the hallway of our school produced by our head custodian. You could have the contest some time before a performance and then incorporate the winner in the show. Dress them up in a Leprechaun outfit and let them carry the tune.

Another option is to simply find one child in your class who can whistle and let them whistle whatever notes come out, or even ask students if one of their parents or grandparents is a good whistler and invite them to class to demonstrate.

The third option, is simply to let the whole class whistle the best they can and celebrate the cacophony!

Get Set...

There are choreography notes over the piano accompaniment on pages 51-54. They are a little more sophisticated than our usual *Hop 'Til You Drop* moves, but not impossible for any age to do. The basic moves that begin in m. 5 involve isolating one part of your body at a time. When the instructions say "Pop your R knee out by lifting your R heel," the only thing that should move is your R heel. Give the knee a good accent. Then, it goes back down and you lift the R shoulder only. Nothing else moves. Then, you lift the L shoulder after the R goes down, then the L knee. So the accent moves around your body.

The Irish Jig is much like the Pony from the 1960s. With hands on hips, hop to your L foot followed by a quick ball-change (RL), then hop to your R foot followed by a ball change (LR). It's a relatively slow tempo for a jig, so you can do the moves in a big fashion.

Loose Leg Swing: simply swing one leg out to the front, then to the back, and then front again before setting it down. It's not too hard.

Go...

Have a lot fun with this song by adding costumes. Red beards, black buckle shoes, white shirts and green everything else make for terrific Leprechaun costumes. Sing this tune and whistle your heart out. Perhaps the luck of the Irish will come to you too!

The Luck of the Irish

Words and Music by
John Jacobson and Roger Emerson

VERSE 1

If you find a four-leaf clover
On your way from Donegal,
You'll be glad your whole life over.
That's the luck of the Irish.
That's the luck of the Irish.

VERSE 2

If you meet a leprechaun
Who's dancing on your neighbor's lawn,
You'll be happy all day long.
That's the luck of the Irish.
That's the luck of the Irish.

REFRAIN

Dance! Dance! Dance! Dance!
Like the Irish do!
Dance! Dance! Dance! Dance!
Luck will come to you!

VERSE 3

If today you're feelin' older,
And your heart is growin' cold,
You will find a pot of gold, for
That's the luck of the Irish.
That's the luck of the Irish.

(Whistle)

REPEAT REFRAIN

REPEAT VERSE 1

That's the luck of the Irish!
That's the luck of the Irish!

9 / 21

The Luck of the Irish

Words and Music by JOHN JACOBSON
and ROGER EMERSON

Place hands on hips with heels together and toes apart

With a bounce (♩. = 96)

D G2/B D/G A Em7 D/G Asus A D

mf

Beat 1: Pop R knee out by lifting R heel — *Beat 2: Raise R shoulder only, R heel back down* — *Beat 1: Raise L shoulder only* — *Beat 2: Pop L knee out by lifting L heel* — *Repeat mm. 5-6 two more times*

mf

1. If you find a four - leaf clo - ver on your way from Don - e - gal,
2. If you meet a lep - re - chaun who's danc - ing on your neigh - bor's lawn,

D G2/B D/G A D G2/B Em7 A

5

Beat 1: Raise R knee and slap it with R hand — *Beat 2: Put R foot down* — *Beat 1: Plié* — *Beat 2: Stand straight*

you'll be glad your whole life o - ver. That's the luck of the I - rish.
you'll be hap - py all day long._ That's the luck of the I - rish.

D G2/B D/G A Em7 D/G Asus A D

9

Repeat m.11 — *Slow plié* — *Stand straight* — *Place R hand over waist and do a formal bow*

That's the luck of the I - rish!
That's the luck of the I - rish!

Em7 D/G A D G2/B D/G A Em7 D/G Asus A D

13

Do the Irish Jig
L R L R L R
Continue to Jig with R hand held overhead
f
Dance! Dance! Dance! Dance! Like the I - rish do! Dance! Dance! Dance! Dance!
C G Em7 A Bm7 Em7 Asus A C G Em7 A
19
L
Stop dancing with feet apart and point from high to low at the audience
Bring L foot in, then R foot in to end up in 1st position
Plié, then up
Luck will come to you!
Bm7 Em7 Asus A
25
1st time: Repeat mm.5-18
2nd time: Loose leg-swing R leg forward, back, forward, down
L leg forward, back, forward, down
mf
3. If to - day you're feel - in' old - er, and your heart is grow - in' cold,
Whistle 2nd time
D G2/B D/G A D G2/B Em7 A
30
Repeat R leg swings
Repeat L leg swings
you will find a pot of gold, for that's the luck of the I - rish.
D G2/B D/G A Em7 D/G Asus A D
34

Repeat R leg swings
Repeat L leg swings
That's the luck of the I - rish!
Em7 D/G A D G2/B D/G A
Do a bow
Repeat mm.19-29
f
Dance! Dance! Dance! Dance!
Em7 D/G Asus A D C G Em7 A
Like the I - rish do. Dance! Dance! Dance! Dance! Luck will come to
Bm7 Em7 Asus A C G Em7 A Bm7 Em7
you!
Asus
A

Repeat mm. 5-12
1. If you find a four - leaf clo - ver on your way from Do - ne - gal,
D G2/B D/G A D G2/B Em7 A
55
you'll be glad your whole life o - ver. That's the luck of the I - rish.
D G2/B D/G A Em7 D/G Asus A D
59
Slap leg again
Plié
Stand with feet apart
and fists on hips
cresc.
That's the luck of the I - rish. That's the luck of the I –
Em7 D/G Asus A D Em7 D/G Asus A
cresc.
63
Scoop R hand low to high
Slap R leg with R hand
with knee up,
then put knee down
Fists on hips
Plié Up
ff
rish! That's the luck of the I - rish!
D G2/B D/G A Em7 D/G A D
ff
68

Walk Faster!

Teaching Objectives and National Standards for "Walk Faster"

- Sing in tune and maintain a steady beat, responding to conductor cues
- Recognize and sing a descant and ostinato
- Identify verse and refrain
- Demonstrate steady beat through movement
- Discuss rhythmic relationships of macro and micro beat

*This lesson addresses the National Standards for Music **K–4** Education: 1b, 1d, 1e, 5a, 5c, 6a, 6b, 6c, 6e, 7a.*

Get Ready...

Now here's a *Hop 'Til You Drop* song that doesn't take a whole lot of explanation. You walk slowly; you walk fast. When you walk fast, you feel better. At least that's my theory and it works for me! So this can be a classroom activity that gets everybody up and moving, or you can use it as a staged number that teaches a lesson to a sedentary audience. To get ready, be it on stage or in a classroom, move all of the chairs out of the way, or at least create aisles through the furniture to make paths for walking. You could approach the number as a "follow-the-leader" type game as you walk in single file throughout the room or about the stage. This would also be a great number to use on the playground or in the gymnasium where your walking could be more athletic.

You might also want to give one or a few performers percussion instruments to beat slowly, then faster and faster as the song progresses.

Get Set...

Another fun way to sing/perform this song is to stand in concentric circles. As you slowly walk, the two circles are moving in opposite directions and continue to do so as you pick up the pace. The teacher, or leader, is given a whistle or some other instrument that can be heard over the music. Whenever the leader blows the whistle, the walkers change direction. When the pace is going faster, this can really be a lot of fun.

It's also a great song with which to play Musical Chairs. As the students walk around the chairs, the tempo of their walking picks up. When the leader stops the music, it can be quite surprising and a lot of fun.

Go...

As a performance piece, there are some very simple staging directions above the piano accompaniment on pages 57-60. The main difference is to keep your bodies (and therefore your voices) facing downstage. The walking and jogging would most likely be in place as opposed to moving around the stage, but it might be fun to have the walkers go up and down the aisles of the audience as well, if you have room.

When you get to the "stack" section at measure 25, divide the cast into three groups: Group 1 – the "walkers," Group 2 – "joggers," and Group 3 – the "wavers." You can simply have them in three groups on stage or, if you want to use the concentric circle idea, have the "walkers" on the inside circle, the "joggers" on the outside circle going a different direction and the "wavers" in the middle surrounded by the other two groups.

I think little children are going to love singing and walking to "Walk Faster," but you might want to introduce it to a few adults in your life as well. You never know...

Walk Faster!

Words and Music by
John Jacobson and Roger Emerson

VERSE 1

When I'm feelin' kinda low
And I can't get up and go,
My life is like a walkin' disaster!
I pick up the pace
And get a smile on my face.
Instead of slowin' down, I walk faster.

REFRAIN

Walk faster. Walk faster.
Just pick up the pace and walk faster.
Walk faster. Walk faster.
Put a smile on your face, and
walk faster!

VERSE 2

I was listenin' to the news,
So, of course, I got the blues.
"Tornado!" said the weather forecaster!
I won't be blown away,
And to find a sunny day,
I'll pick it up and go a bit faster.

REFRAIN

Walk faster. Walk faster.
Just pick up the pace and walk faster.
Walk faster. Walk faster.
Put a smile on your face, and
walk faster!

Part 1 (sing all 4 times):
Walk, walk, walk, walk,
Walk, walk, walk, walk,
Walk, walk, walk, walk faster!

Part 2 (sing 2nd, 3rd, 4th times):
Pick up the pace.
Smile on your face.
Don't you slow down, walk faster!

Part 3 (sing 3rd & 4th times):
Sunny day.
Don't be blown away!

All sing:
I'm walkin' faster. Walk faster.
Just pick up the pace and walk faster.
Walk faster. Walk faster.
Put a smile on your face, and
walk faster!
I'm walkin' faster!
Walk faster.
I'm walkin' faster!

(Spoken Solo)
But no running in the hallways!

Walk Faster!

Words and Music by JOHN JACOBSON
and ROGER EMERSON

Double time the walk, either in place or around the room
fas-ter. Walk fas-ter. Just pick up the pace and walk
A♭7
E♭2/G
Fm11
B♭7sus
Oh,
yeah!
fas-ter. Walk fas-ter. Walk fas - ter. Put a
E♭7
D♭/F
G♭m
E♭7/G
A♭7
E♭2/G
(3rd time) To Coda
smile on your face and walk fas - ter!
Fm11
A♭/B♭
E♭7
A♭/C♯
dim.
sing 1st time only
2. I was
E♭7
A♭/C♯
B♭m/D
E♭7
A♭/C♯
E♭7
play 1st time only

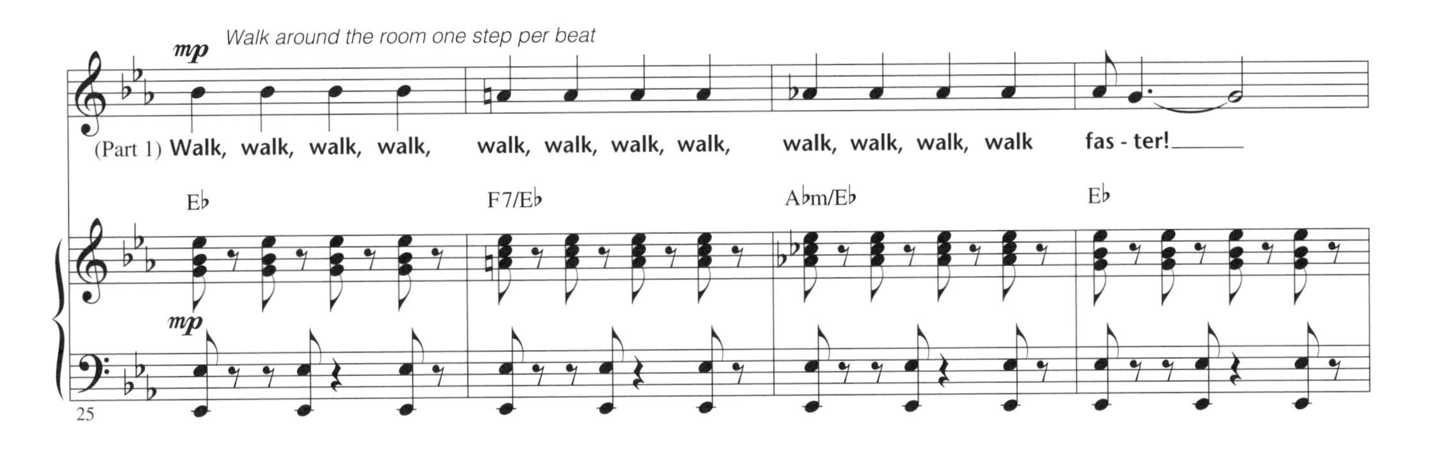
Walk around the room one step per beat
mp
(Part 1) Walk, walk, walk, walk, walk, walk, walk, walk, walk, walk, walk, walk fas - ter!
E♭
F7/E♭
A♭m/E♭
E♭
mp
25

cresc. poco a poco
(Part 1) Walk, walk, walk, walk, walk, walk, walk, walk, walk, walk, walk, walk fas - ter!
(Part 2) Pick up the pace. Smile on your face. Don't you slow down, walk fas - ter!
F7/E♭
A♭m/E♭
E♭
cresc. poco a poco
29

Descant (optional)
(Part 3) Sun - ny day; don't be blown a - way!
Walk, walk, walk, walk, walk, walk, walk, walk, walk, walk, walk, walk fas - ter!
Pick up the pace. Smile on your face. Don't you slow down, walk fas - ter!
F7/E♭
A♭m/E♭
E♭
33

f D.S. al Coda
Sun - ny day; don't be blown a - way. I'm walk-in'
Walk, walk, walk, walk, walk, walk, walk, walk, walk, walk, walk, walk fas - ter!
f
Pick up the pace._ Smile on your face._ Don't you slow down,_ walk fas - ter! I'm walk-in'
F7/E♭
A♭m/E♭
E♭
37
CODA
All walk one step on each beat moving toward stage L
Reverse and walk toward stage R
dim.
fas - ter! I'm walk - in' fas - ter. Walk
N.C.
dim.
41
Reverse and walk toward stage L
Reverse and walk stage R or exit
(spoken)
"But no running in the hallways!"
fas - ter. I'm walk - in' fas - ter!
E♭7 (#9)
f
45

I Am a Great Conductor!

Teaching Objectives and National Standards for "I Am a Great Conductor!"

- Sing in tune, maintaining a steady beat and responding to conductor cues
- Sing a harmony line
- Sing dynamics (mf, f, cresc)
- Compare and contrast known melodies
- Conduct time signatures of 2/4, 3/4 (in 3 & in 1)
- Discuss downbeat, recognize basic rhythms in 2/4 & 3/4
- Develop the ability to evaluate a rehearsal in musical terms

This lesson addresses the National Standards for Music ***K–4*** *Education: 1b, 1c, 1e, 5a, 5c, 6b, 6c, 6e, 7b, 9a, 9c.*

Get Ready...

Did you study the instruments of the orchestra this year? Even if you didn't, I thought it would be a fun idea to have the students become conductors. And who says conductors can't sing as they conduct? Sometimes you're the only tenor! Besides, we all know how much exercise conducting can be. So why not give the students a chance to work it out just like you do everyday? Studies show that conductors live longer lives, partly because of the aerobic exercise they regularly get.

Take some time to teach the students the different conducting patterns slowly. They could use a pencil, drumstick, doweling rod, actual conductor's baton, or simply their hands to participate. Then play recordings of music in different meters and see if the students can figure out which pattern to conduct.

Students can take turns being the conductor of "I Am a Great Conductor" or songs you already know. It's fun (and good for assessment) to have an individual student stand up and conduct a pattern, while the other students guess what meter they are conducting, or name three familiar songs in different meters. Then ask one student to secretly choose one of those and conduct that song with the music only happening in their head. Then the other students guess which of the three songs they are conducting.

Get Set...

Have the students stand next to their desks or in an open spot so nobody touches anybody else. You may stand in front of them and mirror their actions. Follow the choreography suggestions above the piano accompaniment on pages 63-66. If you choose to do the song in a performance setting, have the children pretend to be real conductors. They might wear tailcoats, or even Mozart-style powdered wigs. It's okay to let them conduct a bit flamboyantly as long as it's musically accurate.

Go...

Watch some recordings of famous conductors. Use videos, DVDs or online sources if your school permits. See if your students can tell what meter the conductor is reflecting in his/her gestures. Have your students analyze the other movements of the conductor. What do these actions mean? Does he or she want us to play or sing louder or softer, choppy or smooth?

I Am a Great Conductor!

Words and Music by
John Jacobson and Roger Emerson

I am a great conductor,
So let's all have some fun.
I am a great conductor,
And I conduct in one!

IN THE GOOD OLD SUMMERTIME

Words by Ren Shields
Music by George Evans
("Conductors" conduct a beat in one)

I am a great conductor,
Let me conduct for you.
I am a great conductor
And I conduct in two!

YOU'RE A GRAND OLD FLAG

Words and Music by George M. Cohan
("Conductors" conduct a beat in two)

I am a great conductor,
As you can clearly see.
I am a great conductor,
And I conduct in three!

THE STAR SPANGLED BANNER

Words by Francis Scott Key
Music by John Stafford Smith
("Conductors" conduct a beat in three)

I am a great conductor,
I always know the score.
I am a great conductor,
And I conduct in four!

AMERICA THE BEAUTIFUL

Words by Katherine Lee Bates
Music by Samuel A. Ward
("Conductors" conduct a beat in four)

I am a great conductor,
I always do my best.
We all are great conductors,
Now let's all take a rest!

I Am a Great Conductor!

Words and Music by JOHN JACOBSON
and ROGER EMERSON

Hold a pencil or baton in R hand

All take a slight bow

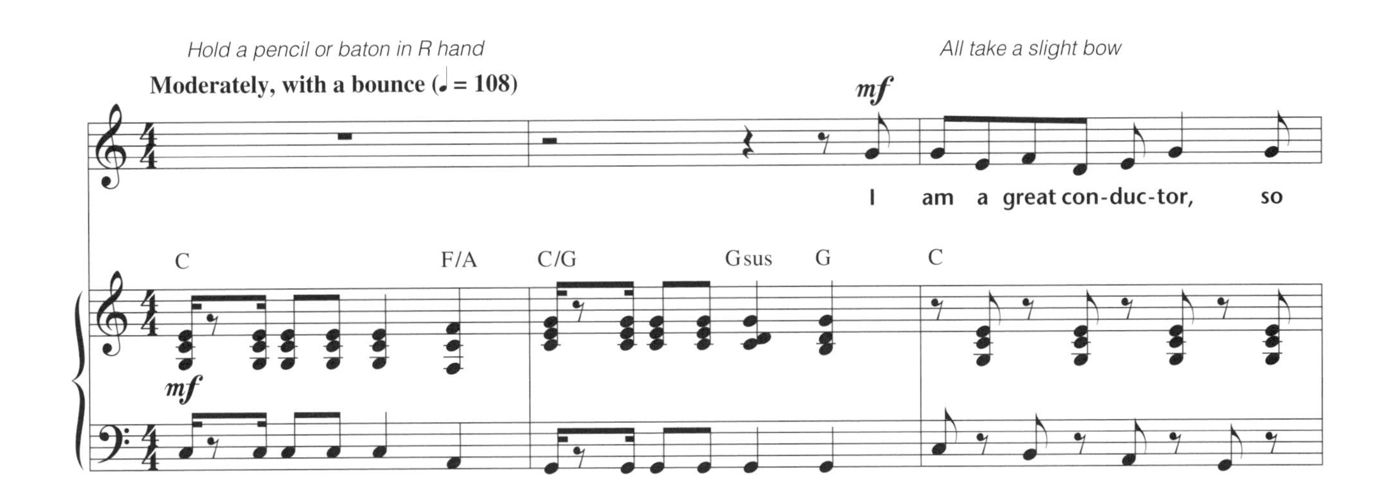

Lift arms as if getting ready to conduct

Conduct a "one" pattern

Lower arms
Moderately, with a bounce (♩ = 108)
A slight bow
mf
I am a great con-duc-tor, let
C
F/A
C/G
Gsus
G
C
13
Raise arms to conduct
me con-duct for you. I am a great con-duc-tor, and I con-duct in two!
Dm7
G9
C
Dm7
G9
C
16
Conduct a "two" pattern
YOU'RE A GRAND OLD FLAG
March, in two (♩ = 120)
F
19
Lower arms
Moderately, with a bounce (♩ = 108)
A slight bow
mf
I am a great con-duc-tor, as
C
F/A
C/G
Gsus
G
C
25

Raise arms to conduct
you can clear-ly see. I am a great con-duc-tor, and I con-duct in three!
Dm7 G9 C Dm7 G9 C
28
Conduct a "three" pattern
THE STAR SPANGLED BANNER
Grandly, in three (♩ = 96)
Arms down
Moderately, with a bounce (♩ = 108)
mf
I
F C/E Dm A/C♯ Dm G C F/A C/G Gsus G
31
Slight bow
Raise arms to conduct
am a great con-duc-tor, I al-ways know the score. I am a great con-duc-tor, and
C Dm7 G9 C
36
Conduct a "four" pattern
AMERICA THE BEAUTIFUL
Grandly, in four (♩ = 96)
I con-duct in four!
Dm7 G9 C C C♯dim7 Dm7 G C♯dim7
39

Moderately, with a bounce (♩ = 108)
Dm7 F/G G C F/A C/G Asus A
I
42
Continue conducting
am a great con-duc-tor, I al-ways do my best. We all are great con-duc-tors, now
D Em7 D/F♯ G D/A A D Em7 D/F♯ Bm
45
Do a big, dramatic cut off
with both hands in the air
let's all take a rest!
Em7 A/E G/A A D D/G♯ D D/G♯ D D/G♯ D/A D
48

Sum-Sum-Summertime

Teaching Objectives and National Standards for "Sum-Sum-Summertime"

- Sing in tune, maintaining a steady beat and responding to conductor
- Sing in 2 parts, maintaining pitch and tempo
- Discriminate between descant and melody lines
- Identify syncopation
- Sing and read dynamic markings (f, ff)
- Develop the ability to evaluate a rehearsal in musical terms

*This lesson addresses the National Standards for Music **K–4** Education: 1b, 1d, 1e, 5a, 5b, 5c, 6a, 6b, 6c, 7a.*

Get Ready...

Since this song is in a 1950-60s pop rock style, we really should incorporate some of the favorite dance moves from that era in our workout. Learn them first and the routine will go together as easy as the Twist.

Get Set...

The 8-Count Twist: The 8-Count Twist takes a little work to master, but is fun and well worth the effort. However, if it gets to be too much of a challenge (especially for the younger "Hoppers"), just do the traditional Twist in a less staged way. To do the 8-Count Twist, start with your feet apart and both hands off to your R.

Beat :

1 Bring your L knee across the front, lifting the L foot off the ground. At the same time both hands move over to your L.

2 Both hands go back to your R as your L foot comes down and you twist your hips and both knees to the L.

3 Twist both knees to the R as both hands move to the L.

4 Lift your R knee across the front as your hands go to the R.

5 R foot comes down. Twist both knees to the R as hands go L.

6 Twist both knees to the L as hands go R.

7 Same as beat 1.

8 Put L foot back down with no weight on it.

Repeat all 8 counts. Note that each set of 8 counts starts with the L knee coming across front, so it is important not to put weight on the L foot on beat 8.

The other steps can be performed in their traditional fashion.

The Pony: Hop to one foot followed by a ball change.

The Swim: Pretend to do different kinds of swimming moves such as the Backstroke, American Crawl, Twisting while holding your nose, etc.

The Monkey: Move both extended arms straight up and down like a monkey climbing a tree trunk.

The Locomotion: Do a combination of heel drags and Choo Choo Train arms.

The Surf: Stand with feet apart and hands held palms down as if on a table, like balancing on a surfboard. Rock downstage and upstage to the beat of the music and try to look like you are surfing.

The Paddy Cake Handshake: Make up a fun handshake with your neighbor. Here's an example: Facing your partner, pat legs, clap, pat R hands, clap, pat L hands, clap, pat both hands.

Go...

If you want to add props, you could incorporate a hula-hoop routine, some could be on skateboards, others could play catch with beach balls, etc.

Have fun. Hey, it's summertime!

Sum-Sum-Summertime

Words and Music by
John Jacobson and Roger Emerson

REFRAIN

Sum-sum-summertime,
Sun is up, so let it shine.
Sum-sum-summertime,
I love my summertime.

Sum-sum-summertime,
Feelin' free, I'm feelin' fine!
Sum-sum-summertime,
I love my summertime.

VERSE 1

Happy days out in the sun,
Camping, swimming, having fun.
Hanging out with all my friends.
(shout) Hope these days will never end!

Lazy, hazy, crazy days,
Ride a wave and catch some rays.
Playing baseball in the park.
(shout) Staying out 'til after dark!

REPEAT REFRAIN

VERSE 2

Plant a garden, take a trip,
Take a dive or take a dip.
Picnics, playing at the beach.
*(shout) No more homework
from the teach'!*

Build a castle in the sand.
This is great, say, ain't it grand?
Daffodils and dandelions,
That's called summertime!
We love summertime!

LAST REFRAIN

Sum-sum-summertime,
Sun is up, so let it shine.
Sum-sum-summertime,
I love my summertime.

Sum-sum-summertime,
Feelin' free, I'm feelin' fine!
Sum-sum-summertime,
I love my summer,
Good ol' summer,
Love my summertime!
Love my summertime!

2 / 24

Sum-Sum-Summertime

Words and Music by JOHN JACOBSON
and ROGER EMERSON

Sum - sum - sum-mer - time; I love my sum - mer - time.
E♭ Cm A♭ B♭ E♭
17
Half a Hand Jive: Pat twice, clap twice
Do the swim
Students: In the sun;
Take a trip;
mf
Leader:
1. Hap - py days out in the sun; camp - ing, swim - ming,
2. Plant a gar - den take a trip, take a dive or
Fm E♭/G
21
Repeat half a Hand Jive
hav - ing fun.
take a dip.
hav - ing fun. Hang - ing out with all my friends.
take a dip. Pic - nics, play - ing at the beach.
A♭ E♭/G Cm
24
1st time: Paddy cake handshake with a friend
2nd time: Wipe a la "safe" in baseball
(students shout)
Both times
Slide L
Slide R
Cra-zy days;
In the sand;
Leader:
Hope these days will nev - er end! La - zy, ha - zy, cra - zy days;
No more home-work from the teach'! Build a cas - tle in the sand.
Fm7 E♭/G A♭ Adim E♭/B♭ B♭ G/B Cm B♭/D
27

1st time: Pretend to swing a baseball bat
2nd time: Pretend to smell a flower

catch some rays.
ain't it grand?

Ride a wave and catch some rays. Play - ing base - ball in the park.
This is great, say, ain't it grand? Daf - fo - dils and dan - de - lions*

E♭ Fm E♭/G Cm

31

Hands on both knees "Oh Toyota!" jump Point R hand at audience

1 (students shout) 2 Leader:

Stay - ing out 'til af - ter dark! That's called sum - mer - time!

Fm7 E♭/G A♭ Adim E♭/B♭ B♭ A♭/B♭ B♭ Fm7 E♭/G A♭ Adim B♭sus

35

Lower hand Clap Point R hand high Everybody do favorite summertime

Students: *cresc.* All *ff*

We love sum - mer - time! Sum - sum -

B♭ Gm7 F/A B♭6 Bdim Csus C F

cresc. *ff*

39

dance moves, e.g. Twist, Pony, Hand Jive, Stroll, Locomotion, Monkey, Jerk, etc. Add hula hoops, skateboards, beach balls, etc.

sum - mer - time; sun is up, so let it shine. Sum - sum -

Dm B♭ F/C C F

43

* pronounced: dande-lines

sum-mer - time; I love my sum - mer-time.
(melody)
Sum - sum -
Dm
B♭
C
F
47
sum-mer - time; feel - in' free! I'm feel-in' fine! Sum - sum -
Dm
B♭
F/C
C
F
51
Face L and hold heart
Clap
Face R and hold heart
Clap
Face front and hold heart
sum-mer - time; I love my sum - mer; good ol' sum - mer, love my sum - mer -
Dm
B♭
C
B♭/D
C/E
B♭
C
55
Do the Twist
Stop and hold heart
Clap X
Present high
time! Love my sum - mer - time!
F
Dm
B♭
C
F
59